DOING WORK WITH SIMPLE MACHINES

WORKING WITH WEDGES

I0812886

RONALD MACHUT

PowerKiDS press
New York

Published in 2020 by The Rosen Publishing Group, Inc.
29 East 21st Street, New York, NY 10010

Copyright © 2020 by The Rosen Publishing Group, Inc.

All rights reserved. No part of this book may be reproduced in any form without permission in writing from the publisher, except by a reviewer.

Copyright 2011; revised edition 2020

Editor: Elizabeth Krajnik
Book Design: Reann Nye

Photo Credits: Cover Noerenberg/Shutterstock.com; p. 6 Volodymyr Nikitenko/Shutterstock.com; p. 7 mareciok/Shutterstock.com; p. 9 Vladimir Melnikov/Shutterstock.com; p. 11 Paradise On Earth/Shutterstock.com; p. 13 Gary S Chapman/Photographer's Choice RF/Getty Images; p. 14 V J Matthew/Shutterstock.com; p. 15 Print Collector/Hulton Archive/Getty Images; p. 16 B Calkins/Shutterstock.com; p. 17 Christina Richards/Shutterstock.com; p. 18 Casper1774 Studio/Shutterstock.com; p. 19 Syda Productions/Shutterstock.com; p. 20 SAHACHATZ/Shutterstock.com; p. 21 sharply_done/E+/Getty Images; p. 22 Africa Studio/Shutterstock.com.

Cataloging-in-Publication Data

Names: Machut, Ronald.
Title: Working with wedges / Ronald Machut.
Description: New York : PowerKids Press, 2020. | Series: Doing work with simple machines | Includes glossary and index.
Identifiers: ISBN 9781538345344 (pbk.) | ISBN 9781538343647 (library bound) | ISBN 9781538345351 (6 pack)
Subjects: LCSH: Wedges–Juvenile literature.
Classification: LCC TJ1201.W44 M25 2020 | DDC 621.8–dc23

Manufactured in the United States of America

CPSIA Compliance Information: Batch #CSPK19. For Further Information contact Rosen Publishing, New York, New York at 1-800-237-9932

CONTENTS

WHAT'S A WEDGE?

Wedges are found in many places, but you might not even know they're there. Wedges can do many things. They can cut, tighten, hold things back, hold things together, dig, and split, or break things apart or into pieces especially along a straight line. Wedges often have handles to make it easier for us to use them. Some wedges are actually two wedges put together, which is called a double wedge. One example of a double wedge is an ax.

The wedge is one of six simple machines. A simple machine is a **device** with few or no moving parts. These devices are used to modify, or change, motion and force to do work.

MECHANICAL MARVELS

Wedges are like inclined planes. Even though they look alike, we use the wedge and the inclined plane for different jobs and in different ways.

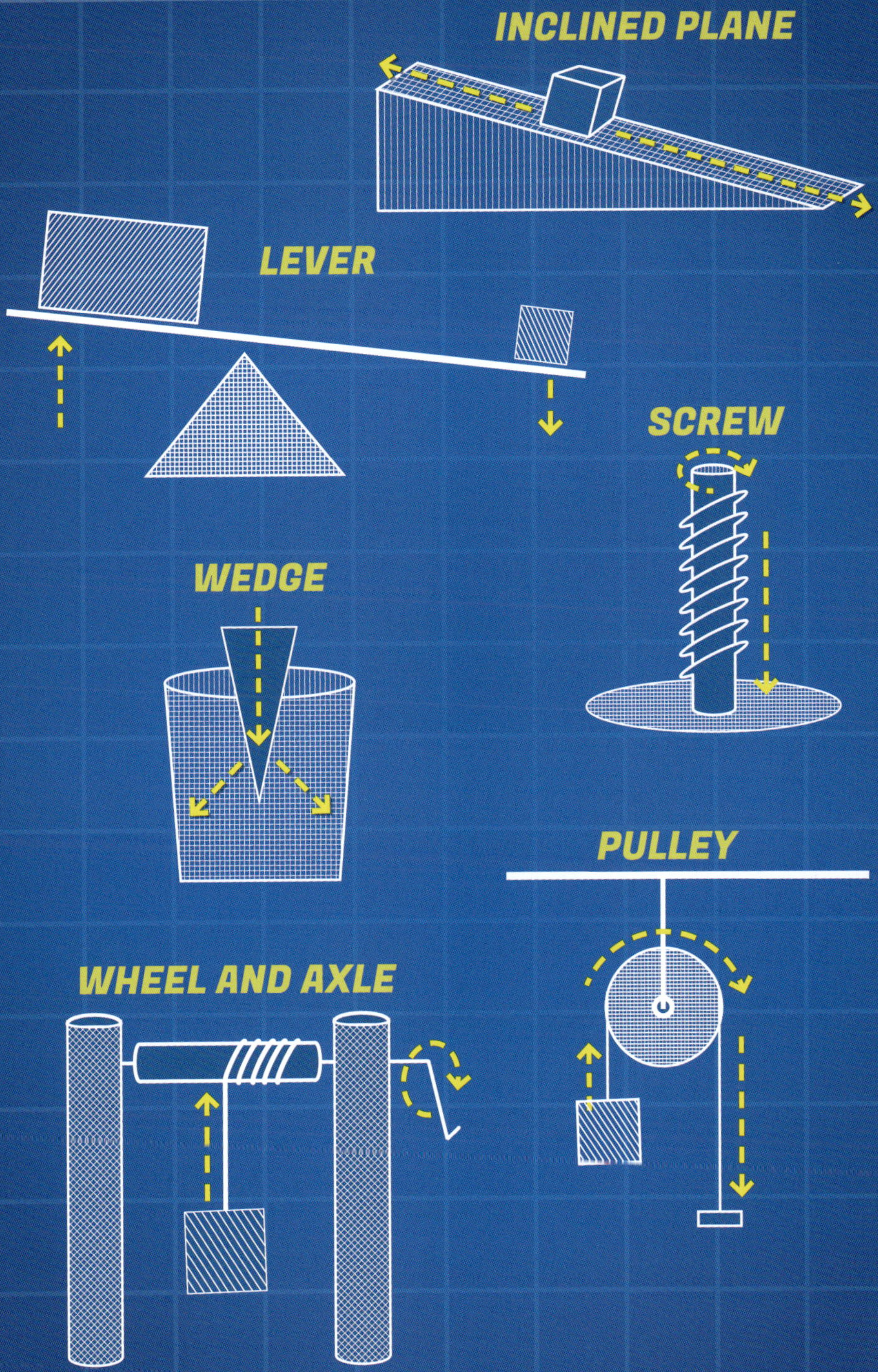

The other simple machines are the pulley, the lever, the inclined plane, the wheel and axle, and the screw.

WEDGE PARTS

Wedges are **modified** inclined planes. An inclined plane doesn't usually move. However, a wedge is an inclined plane that moves. A wedge is a triangular tool usually made of metal, wood, or plastic. One end is wide, but the tool gradually gets thinner until it comes to a point or forms a sharp edge at the opposite end.

A knife is an example of a single wedge.

Wedges that have a handle include axes, shovels, and knives. Wedges such as nails hold two pieces of wood together. Wedges are also found in nature. Your front teeth are wedges that cut food. Even icicles can act like wedges when they fall into the snow beneath them.

MECHANICAL ADVANTAGE

All simple machines provide mechanical advantage, which is the machine's ability to multiply the mechanical force applied to the load. Mechanical advantage makes work easier for us. We apply force to the machine, and the machine multiplies or changes the direction of the applied force. The applied force must be greater than the **resistance** of the object we're trying to cut, move, or hold together.

The longer and thinner a wedge is, the greater its mechanical advantage. A long, thin wedge is easier to use. A shorter, thicker ax may split a log faster, but it means the person using it has to apply more force.

Icebreaker ships have a wide wedge-shaped bow, or front, to force sheets of ice apart and create a path for other ships.

DOING WORK WITH WEDGES

Wedges, like other simple machines such as the pulley, work by changing the direction of the applied force. If **horizontal** force is applied, the wedge converts, or changes, the force to **vertical** force. When a doorstop is pushed under the edge of a door, the force is changed from horizontal to vertical force to hold the door open.

When downward force is applied, the wedge changes the vertical force to horizontal force. When a person swings an ax downward toward a piece of wood, the wedge cuts the wood by changing the downward force to outward force.

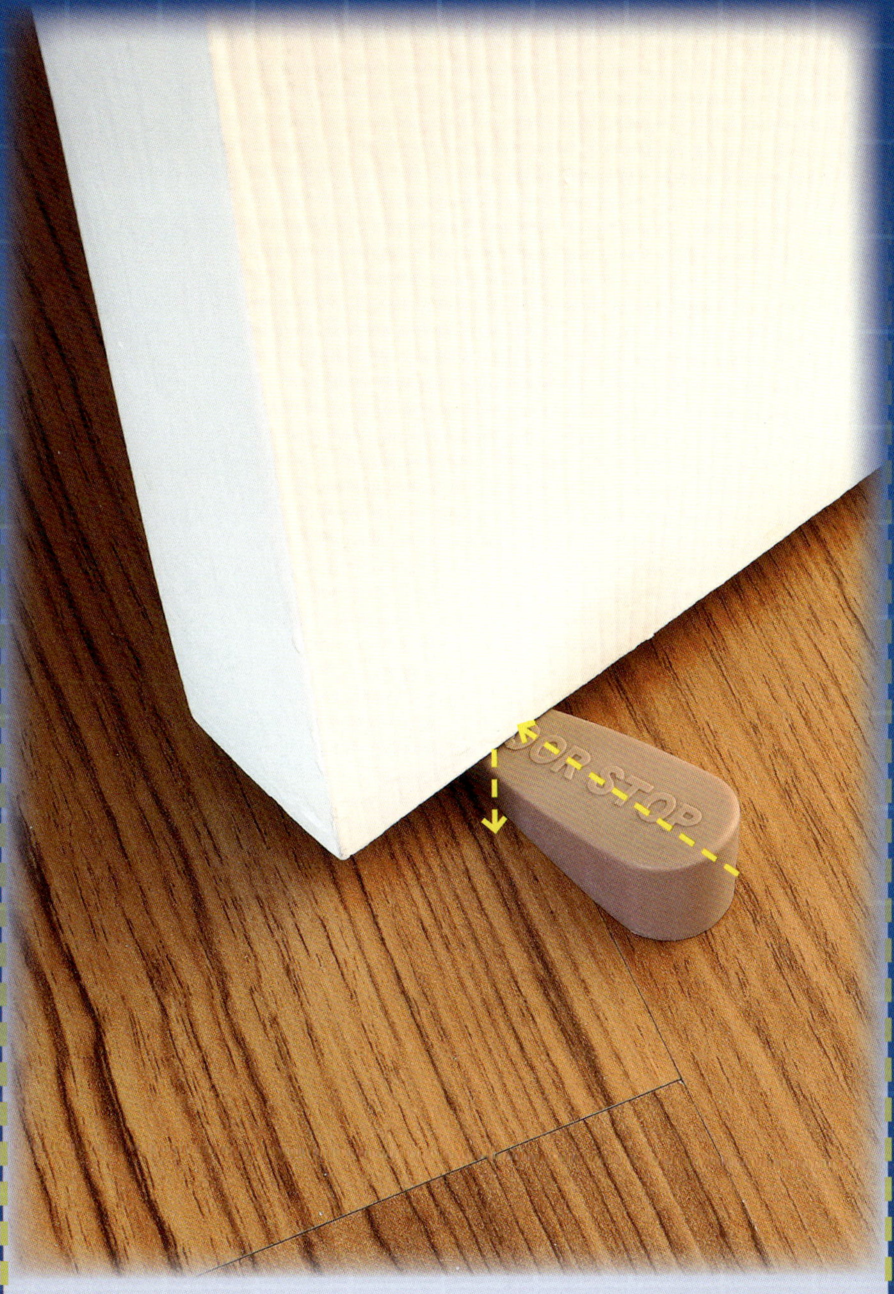

The downward force produced by the doorstop creates **friction** to keep the door from sliding shut.

ANCIENT WEDGES

Wedges have always existed in nature. No one person invented the first wedge. People living in Tanzania, Africa, around 2.6 million years ago used small, teardrop-shaped, stone hand axes to cut and split food, tree branches, and other objects. They made their hand axes by carefully chopping away at one rock with another, stronger rock until the first rock had a narrower edge.

As people learned new things, stone wedges became larger, stronger, and harder to make. These simple machines also spread to different groups of people around the world. **Archaeologists** have found these tools throughout Europe and Asia.

MECHANICAL MARVELS

Scientists think some of the oldest stone tools, which were found on the shores of Lake Turkana in Kenya, Africa, are 700,000 years older than any tools found before. They're older than some of the earliest humans.

Arrowheads are a type of double wedge.

WEDGES IN HISTORY

People have continued to improve wedges throughout history. The ancient Egyptians used metal wedges called **chisels** to dig up many of the softer stones they used to build **tombs**.

People didn't just use axes to chop down trees. They also used them as weapons.

Native Americans used wedges made from animal bone to cut wood used to build their boats and homes. The earliest farmers used large, curved metal wedges, pulled by horses or other work animals, to plow their fields. These plows cut long lines called furrows in the soil and got the soil ready for seeds to be planted. For many years, people have used axes mounted on handles to cut down trees and chop wood.

MODERN WEDGES

We use wedges in many **industries** today. People who work with wood, stone, and clay use chisels. Generally, woodworkers start out using a large chisel to cut away big pieces of wood and then use smaller chisels to shape the wood. Woodworkers also use nails and shims, which are a type of wedge used to make things level or even.

People also use wedges in the farming and construction industries. Backhoes and plows, which are earth-moving machines, use wedge-shaped scoops to cut into and move the ground. Farmers and builders also use shovels to move the earth.

SHIMS

You may find a shim in your home underneath your kitchen countertops. Shims can be made from many things, including cardboard, wood, or metal.

COMPOUND MACHINES WITH WEDGES

Some devices are made up of more than one simple machine. They're called **compound** machines. A number of compound machines have a wedge in them. Scissors are made up of two levers, a **fulcrum**, and two wedges.

Although a shovel may seem simple, it's actually a compound machine. The blade is a wedge and the handle is a lever.

A fan is another compound machine that has wedges in it. A fan is made up of a wheel and axle and wedges. The blades of the fan are the wedges. A zipper is made up of a lever and tiny wedges. A can opener is made up of a lever and a wedge. The handle is the lever and the blade is the wedge.

WEDGES AND AIRCRAFT

Just as wedges can cut through wood, they can also cut through the air. Wedges are aerodynamic, which means they cut through the air and lower the resistance the air produces. For example, the nose of an airplane or jet narrows to a point. This allows the aircraft to go faster and use less fuel than if the nose were flat.

Airplane wings, which are wedges called airfoils, help planes fly. These parts direct air downward and are the most important part of the plane. Without airfoils, planes wouldn't be able to fly.

Four forces act on a plane in flight: lift, drag, weight, and thrust, which is the force produced by an engine that pushes an aircraft forward. As the plane pushes forward, air goes over the wings, which provide lift. Thrust fights drag, and lift fights weight.

WEDGES AROUND US

Wedges are found in many places. A sandbox shovel and a cheese grater are both wedges. A sandbox shovel is used to dig and lift sand. A cheese grater has a perforated surface, which is a surface with many holes. On the bottom of the holes there are small wedges that can grate a block of cheese, or turn it into small slices or shreds.

These aren't the only wedges around you! When you eat, you may have wedges on both sides of your plate. Knives, forks, and spoons can all be used as wedges, scooping or cutting your food into bite-sized pieces.

GLOSSARY

archaeologist: Someone who studies the tools and other objects left behind by ancient people.

chisel: A sharp metal tool used to cut and shape wood, stone, or ice.

compound: Made up of two or more parts.

device: A tool used for a certain purpose.

friction: The force that resists motion between bodies in contact.

fulcrum: A fixed point around which a plank turns as part of a lever.

horizontal: Positioned from side to side rather than up and down.

industry: A group of businesses that provide a certain product or service.

modify: To change.

resistance: An opposing or slowing force.

tomb: A building or chamber above or below the ground in which a dead body is kept.

vertical: Positioned up and down rather than from side to side.

INDEX

WEBSITES

Due to the changing nature of Internet links, PowerKids Press has developed an online list of websites related to the subject of this book. This site is updated regularly. Please use this link to access the list: www.powerkidslinks.com/dwsm/wedges